ITALY

Written by
Hermione Redshaw

TRAVEL THE WORLD!

Gareth Stevens
PUBLISHING

Please visit our website, www.garethstevens.com. For a free color catalog of all our high-quality books, call toll free 1-800-542-2595 or fax 1-877-542-2596.

Cataloging-in-Publication Data

Names: Redshaw, Hermione, 1998-.
Title: Italy / Hermione Redshaw.
Description: New York : Gareth Stevens Publishing, 2024. | Series: Travel the world!
Identifiers: ISBN 9781538288399 (pbk.) | ISBN 9781538288405 (library bound) | ISBN 9781538288412 (ebook)
Subjects: LCSH: Italy--Juvenile literature. | Italy--Description and travel--Juvenile literature.
Classification: LCC DG417.R437 2024 | DDC 945--dc23

Published in 2024 by
Gareth Stevens Publishing
2544 Clinton St.
Buffalo, NY 14224

Written by: Hermione Redshaw
Edited by: Elise Carraway
Designed by: Amy Li

Photo Credits
All images are courtesy of Shutterstock.com, unless otherwise specified. With thanks to Getty Images, Thinkstock Photo and iStockphoto. Recurring images – ONYXprj, Ihor Biliavskyi, alexmstudio. Cover images – Igoror, Sabelskaya, Lebedev Yury, Amanita Silvicora, Rachael Arnott, james weston. 2–3 – bissun. 4–5 – GoodStudio, Darth_Vector. 6–7 – Thoom, gillmar. 8–9 – Garsya, Luciano Mortula – LGM, oneinchpunch, Oscity, trabantos, Alfmaler. 10–11 – ilolab, Mapics, Shebeko, Sky and glass. 12–13 – Seahorse Vector, Sergey Dzyuba, Songquan Deng, Stoker-13, xamnesiacx84. 14–15 – ONYXprj, Dudaeva, Heracles Kritikos, Liubomir_P, Phant, SCStock. 16–17 – Dominik Matus (Wikimedia Commons), LEONARDO VITI, Moloko88, ovalagncy, Sirio Carnevalino. 18–19 – Arthur Balitskii, BAHDANOVICH ALENA, Boris Stroujko, Butter Bites, Darryl Brooks, Takashi Images. 20–21 – CoolR, DaLiu, Gabriele Maltinti, Jenny Sturm, Vadym Lavra, Vector_Up. 22–23 – GoodStudio, alkkdsg, Seahorse Vector.

Printed in the United States of America

CPSIA compliance information: Batch #CSGS24: For further information contact Gareth Stevens at 1-800-542-2595.

Find us on

CONTENTS

WORDS THAT LOOK LIKE THIS CAN BE FOUND IN THE GLOSSARY ON PAGE 24.

WE ARE GOING ON A TRIP

My name is Amelia. Mom and Dad are packing up the car right now because we are going on a road trip! There are lots of things to see and do on a road trip. I cannot wait to get started!

We are going to be driving around Italy. Italy is a country in Europe. Mom and Dad said we will be stopping at some interesting places on the way. I wonder what we will see!

PISA

We start our Italian road trip in Pisa. The most interesting building here is the Leaning Tower of Pisa. I can't wait to have my picture taken with it!

The tower was not meant to be crooked. It started to lean while it was being built because the ground underneath was not strong enough. Dad says the tower will not fall, though. It has been leaning for over 800 years and it is still standing!

GENOA

The next stop is Genoa. This is one of Italy's largest ports. There are lots of palaces in Genoa, called palazzi, as well as museums. We visit the Aquarium of Genoa.

My favorite animals are the dolphins!

SOME BOATS AT THE PORT

PALAZZO REALE

MILAN

A cathedral is called a duomo in Italy. The duomo in Milan is amazing! We go shopping too. Milan is important in the world of fashion. There are many shops inside the Galleria Vittorio Emanuele II shopping mall.

GALLERIA VITTORIO EMANUELE II

THE DUOMO OF MILAN

VENICE

Mom says we cannot go to Venice without taking a boat ride. Venice is built on lots of water, known as Venice's lagoon. The type of boat we take is called a gondola.

Me in a gondola

Some famous artists helped design parts of Venice. There are lots of beautiful buildings here! Our boat goes under Rialto Bridge and past St. Mark's Square, where we see St. Mark's Basilica.

RIALTO BRIDGE

ST. MARK'S BASILICA

BOLOGNA

I thought we had left the canals behind in Venice, but Bologna has some hidden canals. They are hard to find! After that, we visit Bologna's Two Towers. The view from the top is amazing!

FLORENCE

Florence is called Firenze by the locals! While we are there, we visit the Uffizi Gallery. The gallery has lots of rooms filled with amazing art.

ROME

Rome is the capital city of Italy. It has been around since ancient Roman times, so there is lots of history here! First, we have some ice cream by the Trevi Fountain.

TREVI FOUNTAIN

Italian ice cream is called gelato.

PANTHEON

INSIDE THE PANTHEON

Next, we see the Pantheon. You might think it looks familiar because its design has been copied so many times! The Colosseum is another important building in Rome. Gladiator fights used to happen here!

Me in front of the Colosseum

NAPLES

There are plenty of things to see and do in Naples. We see palaces, castles, ruins, and museums. We find plenty of places to stop for pizza!

EGG CASTLE

There is another city beneath Naples. We are given a candle as we go deep underground. Some of the buildings down here are over 2,000 years old! The theater of Neapolis is right underneath the floor of a house on the street above.

POMPEII

Visiting Pompeii is like stepping back in time! In the year AD 79, a volcano called Mount Vesuvius erupted and buried Pompeii. The city was found again many years later. Some buildings look the same as they did in ancient Roman times!

MOUNT VESUVIUS

TEMPLE OF APOLLO

Now entering: Pompeii

SORRENTO AND CAPRI

Sorrento is a town by the coast. You can visit the island of Capri from here! We take a trip in a boat to visit a sea cave called the Blue Grotto. It is amazing!

THE BLUE GROTTO

SORRENTO

SICILY

Italy has lots of islands. We take the car on a ferry so we can see some of them. Sicily has another one of Italy's volcanoes, Mount Etna. It also has the Valley of the Temples, which are ruins that come from ancient Greece!

MOUNT ETNA

VALLEY OF THE TEMPLES

SARDINIA

The last stop on our trip is Sardinia. It takes a long boat ride to get here! Luckily, there are lots of beaches to relax on. We even go swimming in the sea!

BACK HOME

Italy was lots of fun! From Pisa to Sardinia, there were plenty of exciting things to do and see. We saw buildings from thousands of years ago, ate lots of delicious food, and relaxed by the sea.

We did not get to see everything in Italy. I wish we could have seen Miramare Castle in Trieste or the Circus Maximus in Rome. Maybe I will go back again someday and explore more!

Love, Amelia

Ciao!

GLOSSARY

CATHEDRAL an important church building

CAVE a large opening underground or in rocks and hills

DESIGN to plan and make something

FASHION dressing in the most popular way

FERRY a big boat that is used to carry people, things, and vehicles across water

GLADIATOR a person in ancient Rome who fought against another person or animal

RUINS buildings that have been partially destroyed or broken down over time

PORT a place where ships stop to collect and drop off things

VOLCANO a mountain that can form from hot gas and melted rock, which is called lava

INDEX